NEVER BE THE HORSE

AKRON SERIES IN POETRY

Winner of the 1998 Akron Poetry Prize

AKRON SERIES IN POETRY

Elton Glaser, Editor

Barry Seiler, *The Waters of Forgetting*

Raeburn Miller, *The Comma After Love: Selected Poems of Raeburn Miller*

William Greenway, *How the Dead Bury the Dead*

Jon Davis, *Scrimmage of Appetite*

Anita Feng, *Internal Strategies*

Susan Yuzna, *Her Slender Dress*

Raeburn Miller, *The Collected Poems of Raeburn Miller*

Clare Rossini, *Winter Morning with Crow*

Barry Seiler, *Black Leaf*

William Greenway, *Simmer Dim*

Jeanne E. Clark, *Ohio Blue Tips*

Beckian Fritz Goldberg, *Never Be the Horse*

Marlys West, *Notes for a Late-Blooming Martyr*

NEVER BE THE HORSE

BECKIAN FRITZ GOLDBERG

THE UNIVERSITY OF AKRON PRESS
AKRON, OHIO

Acknowledgments

The American Poetry Review: "A Day Passes through the Medium of Identity," "The Gulf," "Never Be the Horse"; *Black Warrior Review:* "Lucifer's Crown"; *Crab Orchard Review:* "Unmeasured Prelude"; *Field:* "Amazon," "Being Pharaoh," "Everything Where I Left It," "The First House Is Burning," "Flowering Adam," "I Have Lived Here All My Life," "I Have Set My Heart on the Sparrow," "Money," "Once a Shoot of Heaven," "Since I Have Lived," "The Ventriloquist"; *The Gettysburg Review:* "Elegy," "My Bomb," "Rebirth," "Refugees," "Swallower," "With a Ravenous Spike"; *Green Mountains Review:* "The Lying Childhood"; *Harper's:* "Refugees"; *Hayden's Ferry Review:* "Retro Lullaby"; *Indiana Review:* "The Suitor"; *The Iowa Review:* "The Painted Adam"; *The New England Review:* "The Betrayer"; *Passages North:* "The Weight"; *Poetry East:* "The Book of Hens," "The Tongue of the Sphinx"; *Poetry Northwest:* "Multiple Adam"; *The Prague Review:* "Multiple Adam," "Refugees," "The Ventriloquist" (reprints); *Sojourner:* "Hound and Leper"; *Sonora Review:* "Sometimes White"; *Western Humanities Review:* "Whitman's Confession: In the Cleft of Eternity." "Being Pharaoh" appeared in *The Best American Poetry 1995,* Richard Howard, guest editor (Scribner, 1995); "Once a Shoot of Heaven" appeared in *Pushcart Prize 1999 XXIII: Best of the Small Presses* (Pushcart Press, 1998).

All inquiries and permission requests should be addressed to the Publisher, The University of Akron Press, 374B Bierce Library, Akron, Ohio 44325-1703

LIBRARY OF CONGRESS-IN-PUBLICATION DATA
Goldberg, Beckian Fritz, 1954–
Never be the horse / Beckian Fritz Goldberg—1st ed.
p. cm. – (Akron series in poetry)
ISBN 1-884836-53-4 (cloth : alk. paper) – ISBN 1-884836-54-2 (pbk. : alk. paper)
I. Title II. Series.
PS3557.03556 N48 1999
811'.54–dc21 99–047169

Manufactured in the United States of America

The paper used in this publication meets the minumum requirements of American National Standard for Information Sciences—Permanence of Paper for Printed Library Materials, ANSI Z39.48-1984. ∞

First Edition, Third Printing

CONTENTS

for Dick

and for my father and mother

What is it called, your country
behind the mountain, behind the year?

—*Paul Celan*

I

REFUGEES

There are too many shoes in the world.
Let's burn them. There are too many
oceans—let's not accept
one more. And let water fend
for itself.

There are too many matches and horses and odometers.
Birds have begun to fly over in boats.
And whatever our hearts are full of they
are full.

Go back.

We have enough bread, terraces, and blue soap.
We have enough starlets.
Our brooms are populous and our roses
need to die. There is too much cupped
and unfolded . . .

There are too many shoes.

There are too many paintings of trees.
Deer have begun to surround New Hampshire.
And wherever our wine spills there's someone
to throw salt.

We have too many satellites and salons and pennies.
We have eyes in front and don't need them in back.
We have six million pianos—

And let windows find their own faces,
there is too much through them at night—

There are too many desires in the world.
Let's pass a law. Too many black ones
and brown ones, tight ones and pink.
We have too much velvet.
There are too many pomegranates.

Go home.

ELEGY

Now the police
come to shoo away the whores from the cemetery,
red skirts drifted in from the streets, into the tall trees,
into the discretion of the dead, their neat countryside.

Someone is always zooming the arced freeway over
the tin and cardboard yards of the poor.

Mother of my country, I'd like
to make a new flag, green with a gray stone on it.

I'd like to suggest levitation as the first right
after cinema baths, always well attended,
because no one's in your shoes,
no one, these days,

capable of understanding the fact that you danced with him,
the fact that you even kissed him, the fact, in the exponentials of
liquory desire, had nothing to do

with the present, its weird thread some neatnik would
yank—everything has to
do with nothing anyone would believe

so simple,
passions. In the most casual degree of lust I admit
I watered

like candles. It's not easy in our time to tell
a mourner by how she's dressed. By the episodic
halations of her perfume, dare of the earring. I just

wanted to go down on Belonging, the only thing, the one,
I was stinging like a slapped child,
like a wasp in the closet, like a retroactive smartness,
the farewell that never got shouted in time—
This has nothing to do with anything I've said or done or

will. What I was dying for was love. What I was loving for
was why was I dying.

MULTIPLE ADAM

There were many made of clay, of straw
in the garden that day, many of flesh,
of gopherwood. Below the orange
lantern-wing of bougainvillea
peacocks had left a fecal scattering.
There were many made of this.
While one Adam was sinking
teeth into the ripe fig, another
ran with the monkeys.
Every story made is made to hide
the others. In the others,
God said nothing
and everything went on as before.
We continued to live in paradise,
our mothers and fathers outlined in the window,
sipping coffee, their lips moving.
And to this mystery-conversation
we can ascribe anything—
as he takes a piece of bread from
her fingers does he ask why, does he
ask where did you get this . . .
All along we have been enjoying
the perfect doze of honeysuckle and
temperate nights and even infinity
like a star cradle. If we have forgotten
it's not our fault. No one can remove
from beauty its confusion, so many
in the garden, and in the middle
the tree of mirrors: It only seemed
desire was everywhere, rebounding
his image like bees off glass,
nostalgias off blisses.

THE VENTRILOQUIST

The voice in me nearly jumping out like wine when
the elbow knocks the cup—I thought surely everyone
could hear it, but I was saved

by the fact that no one listens, each hearing
voices of his own. Each having a nicknamed emptiness, a little dog
kept inside.

How free we are to be shadows then, and
innocent deceivers.

The animals have come down the desert mountains
in the June drought.
No water, comes a voice from the house, from the next,
but they aren't listening—
They are watching the moon slide on its face. It's a fact

I was prayer itself, prayer skinwalking, prayer sinking,
loudmouthed, cursing, dummy on its lap. When I said,
The rosemary gets too much sun, I meant, *Save what I love.*
Or when I said, *My back aches* or *The coffee is wonderful*
or *No, I haven't done much writing lately* or *Is someone
at the door?* or *I could eat nothing but plums the rest of my life,*
or *Not now,* or *Yes, right now,* anything

I uttered was a dry dust off
my lungs. Brown birds walk our bad land's scatter of granite,
beaks parted, mouth-breathers.
I am sorry for the thirst of this world.
Even the world can't drink itself at will.

It must be love it is so like.
The coyote is out on the street thinking, The riverbed has moved.
The actual river is there too, mumbling
Yes, the bed must be somewhere in this valley.

And when a river talks,
you still will not know the fat-child-faith of my heart.

MY BOMB

Better than a dream, it left gargantuan
roses in the Japanese garden, and the rabbits
heavy as children. We would crouch
in the classroom beneath our desks
and concentrate on being small, study
the whitecaps of our knees. Once

we went below the library,
the dark shelves stacked with cans
of creamed corn, green beans, mandarin oranges
we'd eat like the dead for five years
and rise again. Thus,

I learned the catechism: *proton, electron,*
neutron. I learned to contemplate
the Invisible. I went to sleep

in the fire-cloud folding like the brain
and dreamt about the power of my bomb,
girls flashing to the sidewalks, cities
filigreed, the bird-cinders,
light bright as the mirror on the shoe of God

and afterward, pink as phoenixes,
the American Beauties pressing their
mammoth lips to the charge of the sky.
This is how I loved the earth

with my life. With the pure nuclei of
my matter. How it fell into my hands.
Better than desire,
my bomb lit the face of my own

twentieth century. I had it
so no one could use it. I would have more
so no one could have enough.

SINCE I HAVE LIVED

Since I have lived in the desert all summer I've learned
the sound closest to water is the slush of the rabbit
through dead blossoms beneath the oleander.
Next to this, paper. Next,
cars.

I am thinking of the black tongue of the king snake near the shed.
Also the black tongue of your cancered mother—

All the nurses gave us
was a small sponge on a stick
to swab her lips. And finally nothing to do
but tell her, tell her it was all right.

We were devils and angels.
We were wrong, but wrong in the face of helplessness is right.
To do the only thing. And since I have lived

with you, the newly-dead's son. The long-dead's, the
childhood's cut rope. The sound of your sleep is like

sipping the house. The house is dry, dry
and the shortest night of the year is coming
and I'll sleep all morning and I'll take

time and put its one leg in one leg of my pants
and my leg in the other. I'll be alive,
since rising at last is what the living do—

Outside, all down the dry wash rocks spark.
A bird breaks out in the air like a buoyant door.

Which cracks wide my head. Good,
since the ratio of land to water is changing,

and candelabras to fish. Such is wishing, my desert, such
is willing, that for the moment
everything we do metes out
justice. As when the nurse didn't come

my father told me how to insert the catheter
in him, and when he asked
did it embarrass me I said no it did not
embarrass me. For I was at last
given the instruction, given the task to do,
the words to follow, the devil to pay.

The sound of my breath the sound of an upside down cup.

A DAY PASSES THROUGH THE MEDIUM OF IDENTITY

The pine like the wet proof
rising from twilight
does not give away
what century this is. Dusk
cools to a plum of nitrogen.
The birds spread their empire
of melancholic wit. In this,
I could be St. Augustine, Aurelius,
or my own lost grandmother
as a girl humming by the window.

At a universal point
the birds' ecstatic industry
shuts down. I have been wondering
about this for days. Wondering if
we are in the same life—
or if I should curse the house
bringing me such truths. The truth is

I once wrote an elegy for Keats,
having stood in the window of his house,
a museum on the Piazza di Spagna.
There was a lock of his hair
you were not allowed to touch—
the color of balsa or summer
grass. The death mask

lay on the table by his bed.
The window overlooked a cloud
of potted hydrangeas on the steps.
But if you did not look down,
straight out there was only a pure
level of blue, an absolute box
of sky, the kind of view ascribed

to the dead. I told my friend I did not
feel his spirit. And in the very room
where . . .

He could have been the *lamia*
or even a Roman street thief
when he lay in his sick bed and
watched the chalky hour before
morning. The fever was erotic.
The nightingale did not love him.
Its short elliptical breaths
were the effort to raise
his root once, imagining

fat madonnas blowing on
their breakfast fires and air
glassing at the fringe—
a sweat off the spirit
which could be Rafaello, or Autumn,
or Christ: The seed of a man
hotter and briefer
than the dark bitch of poetry.

HOUND AND LEPER

The madwoman in gloves
has let her hand blow open
through soily eyelets, and points
one finger at me across the street.
You're so ugly, she yells.
And in the tinny sunlight I glance
behind me hoping to see
the grotesque. *Where'd you get*
such an ugly face?
She approaches, her blue socks
in rings and a man's shoe
mouthing open at the toe.
I walk on straight and slowly
like my loved ones told me . . .

She shakes her fist as I pass.
A pigeon is whining in the palm tree
and some house with a passion vine
tangles to my left. Will she
follow me, my accuser:
Hash-haired, malty-breathed, eyes of
aluminum and string. At the bridge,
she passes under and I
over the hard crease and quartz,
fossil print of the river
whose mirror has walked. She's seen it,
the disfigurement of dream,
hound and leper in my face—
how flesh is always on
the scent of something, and the marrowy
suck of my eye is creating
symbiosis: Hunger and denial.

It is the one who does not love you
whom you finally believe. Tonight in that
drift before sleep, her voice
is his. On the ceiling, Eros

rides Psyche. I sleep disguised
as myself, my derelict.
Where'd you get that mouth? Christ.
Her eyes hidden behind her hand,
midstreet. My no one.
My confessor. My lips are red iron.
I can't bear their secret.
I'd stuff them with dynamite
and run. Straight home,
like my loved ones said.

I HAVE SET MY HEART ON THE SPARROW

It is as if one set out to love
one of the sparrows flying past and
behold, it has vanished . . .
—*Marcus Aurelius*

One world is always beginning.
The cows meet like the burdens of sleep
in a field, each one
bearing a white part a black part
of the map. I snow

right there, they hardly notice
interference—memory—
They mean to freeze with
their eyes set longingly
on the farmhouse,

eyes like mud trying
to say *love.* Eyes like cows
loving a house, or deciding
smoke from the chimney.

Smoke begins in the belly.
Mother and Father, you are there.
There, this time without me.
I can't begin—

All night I listened to one bird
from my bed, after it had rained.
I said, Imagine there is nothing
to the world but you and the bird—
this one throaty waterfaller, this
small surge, this diamond-chipper. Bird.
It sings. You listen.
It can't conceive of you. You listen.
One bubble in the darkness—

That's where I fell
asleep, where a language
I know only as a language went on
alone. The spilled connection . . .

It's the life again where God
says I can only use three details:
I arrange and I arrange.
I want to be able to say farewell.
I was told once what birds mean:

their calling is only
"I'm a lark," "I'm a wren,"
"I'm a starling, starling, starling."
"This is my territory."

I dream my first memory. House,
I tell the cows
I will love that bird forever.

SWALLOWER

Open the cupboard, cherries rounded up in the darkness.
Sometimes the childhood mystery of the old woman's room.
Its scent bulging out from the polished wooden things,
   from the laciness over which the mirror threw
   back the room, scent wormholing

personal galaxy to personal galaxy. Space is the problem,
the whole
         weep of it. Most of the time. The cherries
themselves, swallowers. All that inked-up redness.
As if the eye-mouth-nostril angel of orifices was
         the only guardian, only

loop into good time. Now

the self is a hundred vigils.
Some of them over bowls and silent bureaus,
some of them over blood-relations, over
that moon over *is this the right bus.*
Then.

Once. I was struck sick while climbing a hill—all
I looked for was a place to heave myself, kneel
and quiver. Even as I approached the feverish
   patinations of my wing-split I knew the trees
   flowering east were tasseling

sheer memory. Its marriages I hate.
The cherries take you
somewhere in you that's out of order: China

dogs lustery on the sill, fleur-de-lised
wallpaper, the rouged-up faces of hand-tinted photographs.
Each face a pulp tightened around a single incident.
How shall I leave the room when I die?

Outside my house the fence wood swells after
rain, the air heavy as fruit. The error is in the equation,
fragrance was a gate upon the heart,
yet only one
    the responsible object.

THE BOOK OF HENS

The wasp wants to be a bell.
This is what I learn in June. I add it
to the things I have confirmed
this year: I am missing.

Here the pomegranate tree has all
blossoms on hold like my dream head—
My mother and father are just married.
My husband and I are just meeting.
He is born.
I am seven, cradling my red dog
for the first time.

I'm the clock with twenty hands.
I am stuck between the past—

Add to this the manuscript I opened
in my studious sleep. I got no further
than the table of contents, titles
my eye ran down:
The Hen Myself
The Rider in the Hen
The Belgian Hen's Monologue to the Tree
I Am the Hen
Hens Eating at Dusk

The heart wants to be—
anything in it.

After the first bite of guilt,
after the dazzling horizon of nakedness
when she was bathing, he saw the skins
laid on the boulder, their fringe,
the downy tips of quail feathers,
folds in the lambskin she tied across
her breasts. He took them to heart
and bound himself, confined the flat-
haloed nipples, caught hairs in the knot.
Feathers flew at his arms and ribs as he
juiced the childish pomegranate against rock,
stained his lips, opened her horn of eyepaint,
fingered the ball-lightning of his lids. It was
like holding shocked wood doves before
their necks snapped. How could he be calm?
He began to pulse as if the woman-bone
buried in him rose, this bitch resurrection
come at last: His new aura, his
plumage, his torchy glances dithering
the lagoon through the red
drag of jasmine, his reflection blinking
back its wounds of earring until his hips
swayed and he danced dressed as Want You,
this masquerade, the flesh
twirled to take beauty
from behind, hosanna, to multiply
a ravishment of one.

UNMEASURED PRELUDE

> Form is but the movement whose form it is.
> —*Jacques Roubaud*

Near a match, what trembles—the world in the palm of your hand,
   gold with red partitions, shifting on its hinges.

Near a door, what hesitates—space, splitting you
   head to foot

and sometimes the scent, when a man passes, holds too much
   information. No angel comes

and clucks its meaning. But listen:
   I read poetry to know a man in France is mourning his wife

to know that someone has also had a theory about shadows
that we dress and undress
that mist hangs in the dripping poplars

   and serious evening comes. Otherwise,

kiss me. Near me,
   what dizzies itself—the wash of sound in the night air after
   the cars pass, the pop-pomp of the boy radio
   the red car pulls farther and farther off

the moment of separation—

To know who had heat. To know the light hairs rising even before
   touch takes its advantage.

Near a field, near speaking.

Near you, what weaves but desire's unmeasured prelude,
   waves, but your own smoke—your breath's sweet onion—

Do not confuse this mouthful with any other.

Even when you see through the lies, the lies they
fed you as a child, you
still believe some of it, still, when you drift
from thinking. When the air's true and simple
like a sheet you've laundered for as long

as you can remember, and your mother before you. There was an end,
and a beginning, and love, and wrong and right and
someone who loved the world and someone who did not
and someone who made the moon and the moon that just was.
Always.

Now there's a white disappearing brow at the edge of September,
usual stars.
   A siren sets off a dog.
   A car radio flies down the road.
   In between, the acacias tick, tick in a lightness not yet wind.

   The early bird is asleep.
   The world still isn't safe for democracy.

There was a mother and a father and a child and an hour
and exactly so many minutes, and left and right,
and people who ascended like doves and people
who slept in the earth, and apples that could make you strong
and sugar that could make you weak, and people who burned.

And tonight you still talk to someone who is not there, not
   yourself—crazy promises, little pleas, momentary

thanksgivings. This no one who has never been there
is like the cat who only went away they said

to live and raise a family in the Christenson's barn. So there was the one who went on living forever and the one you realized could not live forever.

Here there's the sound of a neighbor dragging his trash cans down the driveway to the curb. No one on this street sleeps.
The crickets are poor not lucky.
The ear might as well be gold.

WITH A RAVENOUS SPIKE

I know that city coyote
will take the moon in his teeth tonight,
it's so thin, low,
a pith between darkness and fruit.
Sometimes between the houses
in the last hour still safe from dawn,
an animal scuttle breaks out—snarls,
then the high-pitched yips quick as if greased
from fear. The cat slips through the drapes to the window,
crouches, all hackle. A sheer pleat
rumples against her. How far we've come.
I'm listening as something scuffs away, rattling
the oleander, my past life, ancient Greek life—
not a shepherd, just another girl who stayed awake.
Still, my moods of eternity are brief.
I'll find the torn jackrabbit in the morning.
Coyote, I've heard you come and depart,
even the week I had fever. My ears burned
as if someone secretly desired me, but who
I'd never guess. In my childhood fevers it was
death with cool hands, death who'd singled me out
and I'd lie in my own dewy beatitude,
a hamstrung ache, listening to cars, voices, distant
mowing, oh, they'd miss me. But now I'm older,
now I'm well and the world that goes on around me is
the first one, the one I could only enter
on four legs, with a keen nose, with a ravenous
spike of hunger in my skull. I know that
city coyote has slunk back up the mountain
stinking of rabbit, moon spittle in the rock hollows,
and is satisfied, done with his purpose. Done
with Plato. With Rousseau. With Cartesian nonsense.
He has eaten, enough. He is am.
There is no light yet; a new mint of quiet comes.
Then a three-minute scumble of dream:
Roads again, always roads I've missed
the turn for, roads I'm taking straight up

like the backward film of a waterfall, smack
into waking. Jesus
Christ, the second life no more
whole than the first. If I were let out now like a cat
under the chariots and necklaces and
ladles of the stars—under the bear and swan—
to brush my jowls against some cool nursemaidy flower,
I'd know What For. The moon, my lapland.
I'd know that city coyote as death, testicled
and hairy, one rung above me in the hierarchy
of death as, below me, the rung of rabbit-death, then
lizard-death, down into beetle-death
and the last step off snail-death into
amoebic void. But in this body's slow distinction
to blues, this hour, the east coming out like a scarf
on a balcony, there's nothing but parity—
cars passing childhood and passing now
on the highway, this hunter's hour—a parity of coolness
and hand, dream and ear. Coyote, I return
to my only true subject in light
of desert autumn; no amount of road or house
or urban sprawling drives me out. Though long-winged
memory pursues me: The chick responds to the shadow
of a hawk even before it's out of the shell. And in my bed,
the fever's passing made me wonder if daily a secret combustible
need makes a man quieter, more polite, more
carefully correct, lest he flame—
We are what eats us. Coyote.
The dog-star's fading and the only woman-star
I can name is a burning princess once
fed to the jaws of a serpent.
A story before you sleep. From that dark cave
poked in the mountain, the city is only haze, glint.
The day begins with what
we've left behind. Oh, slowly, I get to my eyes,
face, mouth, shirt, stunned kitchen.
The ground is mantled pink. Quail are walking.

How—do we come back to this
world without iron bands around our hearts
without moon dripping from our teeth, blood
matted in our hair and the one-below-us-in-death
deep in our belly? Oh, I know that sour coyote
would taste worse than spinach and pine pitch,
bitter as the Passover radish. Wafer on Passion Sunday.
But I, like the golden chicken,
butter with cinnamon, rich as the drowned
housefly sipped with the wine.

THE FIRST HOUSE IS BURNING

1

This is the one I would not report.

Radar picks up the heart
and spasms big white islands
across the screen
the glow

tears apart   the shape
jacks itself.

It is my father's heart.
It is the eye nightmare
trapped in the planetarium
when it's closed. I want it to be

autumn when the night's
happened—somehow, while we were
inside. When we entered the building
it was daylight. Stone was daylight
and milk was daylight

a father's milk
safehouse milk
every mouth the welled-up—
the breastbone, field of volts.

2

Outside, windows nub with darkness

But this is the Hospital Cinema

We watch the heart charge
This is the sky

miraculous synthetic
impostor memory
this is my channel

the same bird in the same place in the same
beat: Same
breast j-j-jammed

I am shouting no in the dream's face
even as I make that face
even as I make that face
even as I make my mother
and my father

and that little self-girl
self-goblin   self-angel

so sound comes off like a dust
This is the Hospital Cinema

the keep-sorrow
the aurora
the first house that burns
because we leave it on—

We have gone
and left it on—

If you want more than this,
you want.

3

I have lived all my life as if
talking to one person
who is not there.

Marina Tsvetayeva, you
are not there:

Marina, I have had this dream
that is my life over
and over I have had this:

Why you?
Why me?

Child I have not had,
I am your eyes.

When we are first here, first
in our mother's body
the heart must be enormous
must be a sun dying and dying
must be a rack   a geologic age
a giant moth stunned on   on   on   darkness,
we guess and—

are wrong—
Dear X,

it is autumn. Outside
my open window, leaves fall suddenly
from their hallucination.
I don't hear them till the ground.

Everything is private in daylight.
Help it. Help it.

My young father,

THE SUITOR

In the laboratory they lit me from the inside. They took away
a proof of my lungs, my great moth. I don't know

what they did with. Where is it now that. I go around
breathing but I'm glad
to be a gray cloak and a hat rack inside

the dark foyer of my body with
nowhere else to go. I was the only guest.
I was the only stranger. The suitor, the bearer
   of news.

Though there were ferns somewhere near, sensitive as vein walls.
What I had

was a flash of my own silence, that silence
that could be kept for forty years—
that would outlast my claim on bone,
   blurry organ.

Far in, far in where touch doesn't mean a thing, where I'm
   all science.
Where I live in Thingville. Where no matter which way
the orange is dropped it rolls on its chin, on its chin.
Or when death comes, nothing in its far blind bedroom is nothing.
You just want to be the other end of the gaze of the
   radiated place. Lungs like an apron, heart like an ice chunk.
I wanted to write from the world but I was so alone.

2

NEVER BE THE HORSE

Night on night a horse stood in the hull
crossing an ocean.
It tried to dream on the smell of damp oatseed
its former country, the spongy field
and the clop of a hoof. Later
came winds and a blanket
thrown and a bearded rider swung up
clicking his tongue there in the dark ark's hold.
O they could see dirt roads by the hundreds
vaulted with tamarisks,
the early springs, the breath-apples of winters.
But where were they going—
two sips wobbled in a huge goblet, pitched
and yawed, the constant paradiddle of rain,
doves shitting the rafters. The rider said a voice
had promised on the other side of water
was a green prairie, horizon snug as a rib.
And the horse thought, Never be the horse God talks to.
The waves reached a gallop just
beneath them, reached the horizon and thinned
to sweat, and still
the horse slept upright in the ripe blackness.
Or so they assumed,
the deck passengers, terns, cherubim, archangels, etc.
Months later, a rock rose and then low furzy branches.
Then in each ankle a bell clapped for the mud.

I HAVE LIVED HERE ALL MY LIFE

No, I don't understand my country:
so quiet, grassy, full of ruminant animals,
low light, the thinned volumes of trees.
The chickens dizzy on nectar. I said I'll
go crazy living. Bells walk down
the highway there—I never knew

I was so faithful as a child and kept it all
and believed the first things I saw,
little bell-herder at dusk. Look,

the moon is lost eating and thinking.
And the past needs somewhere to go.

The past isn't big like the world but small
like the Urals. Like Hungary—
smaller—barely wide enough
to keep the buzzard of my right ear
from the doe of my left . . .

You know in America they
won't let me write like this.

The child on the highway
shoots the child in the yard.

I don't understand the night here,
the crickets' tower where the rope
won't stop swinging,
dictators, dictators everywhere:
Everything must leave me.

Because the moon is in my face the birds go blind.

AMAZON

Yellow cotton with its printed leaves
green burns around the eyes of parakeets,
my mother brings me the dress
I used to live in. I pin
its small shoulders against mine, the hem
blossoming a precise border above
my hipbones. Mother, what can the world
do with this dress if you don't know?
I spread the hand of an Amazon
over its narrow chest, folding
easily as noon shadow. The moth in my closet
has disguised herself as a brooch.
On the dim shelf, papers, a sombrero, a toy
mandolin, wait for the boat

to the next world. I cross
the sleeves of the breathless. There
with the blush of the laundered, seam of
half-flowers, the faint ozone of ectoplasm
rises—the female golem. She's afraid
of children. For after children,
what next—

hand-tracings, starry schoolwork, ancient
valentines. White shoes in my palm.
I'm too enormous to live. Oh, time

is the one we can't do to
what we want to. Mother,
I'll be the one.

EVERYTHING WHERE I LEFT IT

I go to another bed in my dream.
At the foot of it, the dog
doubts me with his one blue eye,
knows me with his one brown.
One minute on the radio clock
glows into another. Beside me,
fisherman, you murmur when
your wife will be home. I'll be gone—

like happiness. And then,
in twenty years, come
back to bed. Do you remember me?
We met once on the streets of Haifa,
you carrying a bag of sunflower seeds,
spitting their hulls onto the pavement.
We walked till dawn—

a hyperviolet sweeping the bay.
I go to another sea now, crests
of the ragweed outside your house.
The windows soft as hems. But nothing

binds memory to memory, nothing
explains where I wake
and have you buried him, you
must have, but when—
the lean gray dog

who clicked lightly to the door
and back when I stirred. Over his skull
the cool fur tightened, the way
a wound heals up. . . . This

is what startles me.
In all this loveless time, I had
never dreamed
he could not still be with us.

THE BETRAYER

I dreamed a betrayer
sat with you behind the door—the betrayer
gleeful and you
cool, determined to shake off
my foolish shadow
lurking in the hall: Little Heartsick,
the devil's sparrow.

In the other dream, you were kind
and sat down beside me where shade
laced the grass, and touched my face,
smiling—as if it had been forever,
as if in another world where
our thoughts make it out
alive—

For a while I walked around
with a dream on each shoulder,
the good monkey and the bad monkey,
which was loss and which was loss . . .

For a while I walked around,
my eye dark
as the deep tooth gone—
until I knew them as my equals,
the mind hunched in the mind, darkness
taking every form for love.

THE LYING CHILDHOOD

I am Bluecrest and the ogre.
I love climbing to my window.

I am my mother reading the story.

I am Memory sleeping with her voice.

My tears turn to sapphires.
I am the Rescued and Not Rescued

by love. Oh, I'm True Love
with his thick claws dug in

the Stone Tower—I am a night
coming in again, again like a thin

sealed envelope under the door
shut upon a time. I'm the Dreamy

Ear, the swirl beneath
my eyelids. I am Fair One

and Dark One, the restless
sympathy bird who flies by

like a stuffed keyhole, a piece of
the guard. I am the guard.

I am Bluecrest. I am hair the color
of nuthatches. I

am what happened then
and then and then. Window,

read me: the Blissmonger,
the Hunger, I am

Long Ago. I am Maiden-Junk.
My sighs trip into perfume.

I am moon like the top off
the house—I am

the spark-appalling nimbus-headed
angel, the Lying Childhood,

the father snoring, the car
with rain-tails.

I am the closet, handless,
footless,

breath's pocket. Get me back.
My name is Bluecrest. I live on

this avenue. Fear
on Diamond.

SOMETIMES WHITE

The house is sure I will die.
When I shut it up
in summer with its bald oven,
with scent, the phantom, and the bed's
malingering—it sits above
the desert like a countenance.
Evenings, I sit on its blue lawn,
trying to determine which
is its real eye.

Sometimes white
with pink sills, it's
the child house—
a bat flies in,
my mother bakes my clay hand,
my sister hums with a clarinet . . .
sometimes

white and umber,
the crickets die in goblets,
we drink wine, our exhausted
limbs pool in the laundry,
my mirror burns late—

Late afternoon when an airplane
makes it think, midnight
when I bring nightmare
for a glass of water—it is sure
as blind love
of my absence tossed
on each bed like a coat.

Sometimes I put on its sleeve,
cannot find the other, turn
around and around, my house, my own
house, my own mother, my lamp
putting down on the desk its
own round book,

the book of comforts, the book of hands,
of backs. I am not sure I will die,
space a bell over my ears.
The house is so literal,
it lights me.

WHITMAN'S CONFESSION: IN THE CLEFT OF ETERNITY

. . . look for me under your bootsoles.

What happened was my last breath fell back
on me like pins, the Ultimates—
and my hand slushed through
my chest into stars: None of you
mattered anymore, my nipples pointing off
the sawgrass and your faces all
dooryard. I did not wait for you long.
When the body was gone, there was not even perfume.
There was a suck

like a choir about to and then not. I
tell you of the kosmos, vast puke
and scintillation. We do not go anywhere.
And when my eye studied
the catechism of the image, it went: Worm,
nest, bridge, reflection, stripe rolling over
into worm. What happened was they

struck me with the bomb of the Buddha,
all the multitudes from the top of my head and from
the ribs' shoelace. I withered firsthand, text,
translation, emanation, ink, and rag
into the cud of the Milky Way, thrush-
bone and mule-bone
wheeling in the dander-fields and through
the clean bowels of Orion
turning over me the blue straight-

hairs of the diamond. *Is this then a touch?*
What happened is I lost the animal of my likeness,
Earth of fur—
Earth of legitimate odors and of nights arm-in-arm.
I no longer know who set the woman on that road
or how her face can shape to what is missing.
I no longer know that the clasp of a man

is the cuttle of my vibrations.
Or that the lapidary of distances is memory—

Or that milk is cold.
You will not find me in any energy,
the tender, the gross, the metastasized, the skittish,
the thralling, the angelic. I hit the Void
running, and it was easy to betray you.
I could not wait for you. The poem
was the god who only yearned
to fuck alone.

MONEY

It is wrong to stay here and talk forever, the sack of thunder
over the black mountains still cinched, a shudder

and a batting of violet. The late monsoon wanders, nods off.
The nights clear and the stars know where to cut.
I have not moved. The voice wheedles out of its smallness
fondling each pitch, up

against the thigh of some death. Who can understand
the misery of the finch—this one

summer just ebbing has been its whole year,
the first coolness, the first mother-death, time's so
bird-fast.

And I, I who was born with a fascinated tongue,
sit bare-kneed in the eclipse. The moon

coppers until its cradle cap—so white—slips back
to be the strange chip Mongolia must see,
its people just rising—that mirror hour

fainting into frank blueness. Knowing two things at
one time is the endless money of the distance,

and the dream of a perfect match
for your mouth, your nature, your breeding season,
is your

crush on the down of night, the fall
coming. I wish

to be hunted and found, and found, shot, and
shot, rocked with grief and bandaged, and bandaged,

given time.

THE WEIGHT

I dragged my father in my sleep,
held him up, his arms and legs dangling,
cheek on the bone of my shoulder,
and let him stand, naked,
as if boats were upright,
as if women had entered
his room—

then there was the watching, whole
minutes of it, whole time,
enough to escort my childhood to
its window and to see him always
wandering near the table
speaking to strangers, and time here
to insert the proverbs of my mother:
Men are the dreamers,
women are the real things—
and the madness of my grandmother
who said one day: *There's a bird's nest*

on the stove. If I were a light,
I would not choose to light up the darkness
this way, but he was so unfamiliar
with balance and no one minding
his nakedness, I kept my eye

like a tree over the water
and I am sure he did not know
I was there, as if this were his
childhood or the other life
where we do not meet, do not
love who we love and yet love,
just as much, who we are . . .

I was like the candle flame tossing
some remembered weight, a thimble
of nearness, of nearness
as he moved from conversation to
conversation, eating the wings and grapes,

the small handfuls, the salty things,
sipping the ice-bells and alcohol, being thin
ready to sway—
a candle throwing tigers

or drawing emptiness like a finger
and keeping it there, in the daring
blue threshold—
long enough, perhaps, to recall here
the words of my brother the soldier:
There's no such thing as time you know
you go in figuring you're already dead
there's no such thing . . .

What is it then I go through
dragging the dream—what has been
this immense ever since
God slept with Memory? Time here
to ask why I hold a life not
in my arms like this: like a simple
space, like a lake
in which the sky stands up
the other way,

letting the doubles love. But only a night
is domed in me, bottles and almonds
and guests carrying plates
lightly from politics to music, murmuring,
as I drape his hips with a white cloth.
As I touch hesitation. Then
there was the future. There was then—and then
only the fear my breath
would bell his fall.

LUCIFER'S CROWN

I

He dreamt of an apple big as a house,
of a snake smooth as tears. He dreamt a mine
opened in his pillow, plutonium
crouched inside the pitchblende, an opal
in the bowels. Before, all his dreams had been
of falling—that sexual vertigo—
of windflowers between his ears and his
belly dropping out like a wine jug through
a wet paper sack. He was simple as
a man who in his loneliness believed
everything in a different room
of his heart, a master politician
for these, the troubled times which now were just
beginning, now that God had left his bed.

2

Beginning now that God had left his bed,
he put on a beard of glittered nightsweat,
the musk of the oryx, iridescent
pigeon-ring, stockings of the panther, yet
it was no use—each form an extension
of his discontent, until the dream wound
back to him and he put on the slick tongue—
until his body was a mind turning
into itself, its wonder-twister, its
who am I, its why, its wanting over
and over, its loopy memory . . . Now
snuffed of every grace but talk of it,
the beginning was the word and the word was
flesh, flesh became the world and he was it.

3

Flesh, flesh became the world and he was it:
The garden odors were like his staircase
fallen, clove on jasmine, on shaved cedar,
on punk loams, on mineral gladness. So
he descended. In her depth, the woman
was alone. The rake dropped behind her. He
tried to say something with leaves. Then he swirled
up and kissed her. It wasn't that he was
beautiful and brilliant, a nova of
mothers-of-pearl, but that she could smell on
his breath, already, the death camps, little
incident in Armenia, slave ships,
Prague Spring, and she loved his small mouth full of
gossamer gibber, that heavenly French.

4

Gossamer gibber, that heavenly French
spinning endlessly from the spider sac
between his teeth, swan-necked syllables, quenched
consonants and vowels, round Cadillacs
of sound, his whisper's plush upholstery
where her ear curled up, morphemic mysteries
with seven veils and seven gold lit wicks
in oil behind them, *burnt lark, burnt heart,* she
began to lip-read him like fire, mimic
light lost, light lost—poor blackballed angel, he
waved and said Let there be, and there was not.
There was evening, and he could not rest
his voice, still his quick fricatives, stop
the one thing that made him more than a beast.

5

The one thing that made him more than a beast,
less than a star, let him charge the holy
atmosphere unnoticed except that birds
would freeze a moment and moths would dash him.
And less than a newborn bomb let him drop
at her feet and roll, this smart of matter
known as the Evil One, Prince, Fiend, Old Scratch.
The one thing was he could articulate
his silence, the way a homesickness must
sound the past or a dark lust ventriloquize
the present. More than a lover, less than
a friend, he sweet-nothinged her: *Here we are,*
oh, Eve-bird, this our human fate, to be
in paradise longing for paradise.

6

In paradise, longing for paradise,
each leaf loved its pointed face on the calm
water and fell for it. Each grape in its
cluster loved its shadow on the other.
Each thing stood its tiny doll on its head
in the dark of his eye and his reason
righted it. Thus he practiced like the world
small tricks to order his memory. But
each time he succeeded, chaos increased;
each epiphany used more fuel than
it gave. For two lights must go out for one
to go on in memory, and the mind
in desiring undress down to its horns,
lock with hunger, knock its back to earth.

7

Lock with hunger, knock its back to earth,
it was no angel glorious like he,
but it would do—the demon's demon, yes,
the spitting in his own image. Drown it.
Mourn it. Sex it. The soul, apoplectic
blossom. How beauty would craze him who could
not hold it, though the mere sight of the moon
would nearly crack his loins. Smother it, nail
hit on his own head: He was the woman
inside the woman, man inside the man,
the blackbird alive in the pie. Eat it.
Sleep. Simple as a child at night who dreams
it's light, he was light. Fallen. Rockabyed.
And rolled back the apple of his big eye.

RETRO LULLABY

Sometimes I carry the smell of moist hay from my childhood.
And sometimes I put down this burden, never
without its consent. Long have I

known memory and willingness to be one fold,
though I find it difficult to talk to my childhood
since I had the flying dream—my robes

bubbled over the desert—
And now all I have is a postcard of a little stranger.
If I drop the card in the hay-smell,

her ear will plump up like a dried apricot in wine.
And her stupid white hands will come up like two
white pages from the bottom of a lake

And I'll coo, It's ok, you can be my baby.
My part.

I can never remember the whole day.

After all, my sister said I was a strange child, an
automaton.
My mother said if they talked idly in February
of going somewhere in June, I'd wake in June,
my suitcase packed.

Terrible she said to have a child who never forgot a thing.

But now, of course, I've slipped
my mind forever in some infeasible way, flown

stiff as a toy in my dream altitude and I remember
wondering even in my elation if I'd drop
suddenly and if I did

I don't remember. But if I did, I'd say,
It's ok, you can be my angel. You can be
my human kite.

At any time, we might give in. Just a knuckle of us,
    or a cheek. Because the
    ferment of the hayfield unpacks on the side of a road
    and one second

gets the Gone going again, her little hairs stand up.

And childhood stinks big in our lives as death.
And in between is willingness—her tongue comes out
    speaking its *motherese*—

All right. You can be my lake, my June, my hay-fish.
    Be my keen hound. My. Love of My Life.

THE GULF

There were seascapes above green couches.
In the first darkness, we would walk past
the houses. Their hearts were open.
A child lived there sometimes or a man sitting
some distance from his shoes. And the wave
about to crest, transparent
like the blue-green above
the stray dog's backbone at dusk.

After three nights, we were sick
of watching the war. Luckily,
it was very far away: My dreams beside yours
then yours last night beside last summer's
then last summer's beside your mother's
who is dead now.
But the world is still in its own.

On the shore, the oil birds
stagger like rubber knives, and deep
boots of wine. And a carp floats
like just the lung of a young girl.

At night it feels as if we are
in the eye of something. If we want to stay
on earth, in love, no matter what
governments do, we'll have to take in
each rock, each dog, each wing to
our houses. See what is not true.
A fish is not a girl.
A bird is not a man.
A man can say when he is a man
and when he is not.

A wave sludges to the shore.
The sea is black.
It is black and it is close
as the pupil of heaven.

FLOWERING ADAM

When he thought he was crazy, when he was
crazy, when he was dead, when he thought

he was dead in the earth and eaten
and corrupt, when he was swarming and

desiccated and hellholed in his sockets, old
eyeball rolled in his gullet and something

working, working under the green
pinlight of his breastbone, when

it came to this—unhinged in his body—
he rose up dry as the cicada,

he rose up by limestone, root and sod,
Adam Stinkweed, back in the black garden.

It was all char and incense.
But he had risen. He was dead

crazy as that star shook and milky
spokes walked between the grass—

He rose up Lily-of-the-Valley.
He rose up nipples in his palm,

Adam Erectus, without the sensitive
root of the living. What bird

could he scare from the field?
Where could desire thrust him then?

He could not imagine for all
the eunuchs in heaven why he

would return as the beggar of form,
a wickless candle, a gifted vegetable

parlaying dung into sweet air . . .
He would stick in the teeth of cows or

pass through the rabbit: Destiny—
what man doesn't find it in the waste

of his heart? With no eyes but blossoms
to see he was good, he blossomed

orange as the hackles of foxes, orange
as the lucifers of magma, burning

petals like wings shot and gilded
hesitations—like the crown

of the carrot above the dream's poor
writing finger, he blossomed and let go

seed to second honeymoon the soil:
fly trap, thistle, watcher-by-the-wayside,

a quince tree, blushing, and from its branches
golden death's balls hung

above the spoonbush, above the tongue bramble,
Adam Succulent, Adam Rose,

jacked in the fiery pulpit.

THE TONGUE OF THE SPHINX

for Rick Noguchi

What's the difference
between grave robbing and poetry?

It doesn't matter how you found it
but that you dragged the old
porcelain commode to the middle of your yard,
shining, useless, to your back window.
In the afternoon, you said, it looks friendly.
But at night it's the Blue Morpho, a stare
into the terror of objects.
I said, Some night watch who comes
and sits there:

the grocer from childhood, the ancestor,
the loved one's ignominious death—
I meant this for you, but I was haunted,
and what the moon lit was that white
open, your absurd muse. And your
most private. Wasn't it Stevens who said
resist

the pressure of reality? Wasn't it Freud
who said all children
believe their shit is precious? Think

what relief is there for our lives,
for the lives of those who love us
when we are always watching—
as if otherwise their nakedness
would go to waste. I want you to hear
my confession: I saw my father stricken
and wrote it down. I saw my husband's
darkness and I wrote it down. I saw
his father leaned against the bathtub
with his soiled trousers undone, weeping
and his wife gone and his house sold

and the nasturtiums they planted still blooming
and I wrote it down.

What's the proper punishment
for stealing a life—a hand   two hands
a hand and a foot?

Look, tonight,
who is out there. Someone who wants only
some time to read, some time alone—
someone I love,
someone whose eye is like the burn-ring
in the gold poppy . . .

Use him, use him if you can.

For what is the difference
between thievery and love?

REBIRTH

One summer I saw the old wing
of the hospital where I was born—in the windows,
stacked boxes of cleanser, disinfectant.
It stared at me like an old brick warehouse.
It stood in the middle of a field.
I was startled by the bored look of it
as a woman by the distant
expression of a lover. We slowed
past on the road as my mother told me
it had been snowing, a May blizzard that evening
and the very road
down which I had no memory—
this humid August and a day moth's
fibrillations over ragweed over sawgrass.
I said my first light
was on the cellar door open and the hammers
ringing: Father sawdust shadows brothers
and that echo wowing the spring air.
She said I came out dark-haired,
a good sleeper.
I said it was
the chickens walking under the lilac.
She said I first moved when the town band
played a concert in the park.
She did not say *the stars were clear and close*
as the lashes of the ecstatic . . .
And I did not say *the night moved in rings*
like blood fielding a trumpet.
The windows were dimming in rows
like schooldays. Or that part of our life
only someone else remembers. I said
my first love
was autumn sky lost in the empty
corncribs and the cows steamy and lonely
without end. She said
I was born happy.

BEING PHARAOH

My grandmother turned into an old man,
deaf, with a hairy chin. It is August,

the damp panting of nights—I am
gradually building my own underworld

not just with prospective grief but
wires to hold up the asphodels.

Into it, a whole migration of shapes
skinned by light, pears gone

flat, and cars, and shadow like a floored heart.
They're the file of a river

and the Greeks had a river, the Romans.
The Egyptians who civilized the dead.

Tonight I am sick of every man
and his past. And the past is tired of his

request that it love him. I am trying
to make my bed. I am trying to keep

an angel from cracking my hip. The moon's
sleeve is flipped back in a drawer . . .

Thrush, you little singing spade—
I'm an unforgivably domestic mourner

and I might sleep through someone's
late supper, or hunger—just think how

oblivious he will be. While I am in
the dark rustling my own inventory:

Each time we fall out of love we
say it wasn't really love at all as if

landing, a plane would say *no, not
actual sky.* While I am in the dark

getting fit for an afterlife. Admit
we never know the difference, like the woman

who stands up in the cinema and becomes
the black keyhole we peer into. I am

trying to keep her head down. So long
even her mother and mother's mother

turn blue. I am trying to keep
the ancestors out of the bedroom

so I can conceive a new face and new
arms, the feather trees across

the river, the curious shore dog.
Keep the distance simple like the top

deck of the parking garage from which
we can see the hospital. The present

may bond to any molecule, future
or past: My parents were kissing

while someone dragged the body past
the doorway, bag zipped to the chin

on the gurney, the head wound in white gauzes.
My father had taken off his mask, still

hissing oxygen, and mother was bent.
Of all things I've seen it was

old love that kept them from seeing.
Beautiful discretion, what moment will you

save from me? This should have been
a dream, something to wake from

but I never do. I am trying.
I will be pharaoh yet—

sealed with tiny boats and slavish
figurines. I am sick of every face

floating a sex by itself. Take in
this lampshade and these

curtains. Objects are memory.
As a child, I pictured the soul as a glass

wing, fluted, gelatinous, detached
as my voice under water. I made it up

a body—a paperweight—no snow
in the water, no water under the earth,

no music ever again in my hair, after
my hair. The dead will point to it,

What was the name for this, point to my hand,
What was the name for this? One life

has been mine so long, streets
and bicycles, monuments

descend in it. In the bedroom, a shirt
has fallen on shoes. Keep me

from seeing: Moon wanting into the dark
like the torn from—

the photograph—
It is August. One woman is so long

longing does not come out of her.
But this time I have loved you

so long I become
the boy you were. I must still

be alive, for everything is changing and
incomplete. Half a tree, half

drives its shadowy web near the shutters.
August has just turned September. The ancestors

want 4000-year-old grain, hard as quartz,
in grain jars. All I have are cigarettes.

What a night this is. What a night.
I'll lie down and my pillow will thrum

like a machine. I'll go barefoot
to the window, see if any light is

still on in any house. Who else
is afraid of missing something. Who else

knows one thing God can't enter
is my memory: I, a minor

twentieth-century poet, the first
of September, 4 A.M., finish one thing.

ABOUT THE AUTHOR

Beckian Fritz Goldberg is an associate professor of English at Arizona State University in Tempe, Arizona. She received a BA and MA in English at Arizona State University and took an MFA in Creative Writing at Vermont College. Goldberg has previously published two full-length collections, *Body Betrayer* and *In the Badlands of Desire,* with Cleveland State University Press, and her poetry has appeared in numerous journals and anthologies, such as *The Best American Poetry 1995* and *Fever Dreams: Contemporary Arizona Poetry.* She has received several prizes for her work, including a 1998 Pushcart Prize and the *Gettysburg Review* Annual Poetry Award.

ABOUT THE BOOK

Never Be the Horse was designed and typeset by Kachergis Book Design of Pittsboro, North Carolina. The typeface, Bembo, was based on typefaces that were cut in 1495 by Francesco Griffo for Aldus Manutius' printing of Pietro Bembo's *De Aetna*. Bembo is considered one of the first old style faces that were used over the next 200 years in Europe. Stanley Morison supervised the design of Bembo for the Monotype Corporation in 1929.

Never Be the Horse was printed on sixty-pound Natural and bound by BookMasters of Ashland, Ohio.